LALO

SYMPHONIE ESPAGNOLE

Opus 21

FOR VIOLIN AND PIANO

(ZINO FRANCESCATTI)

INTERNATIONAL MUSIC COMPANY

5 WEST 37th STREET   NEW YORK CITY

SYMPHONIE ESPAGNOLE

Edited by ZINO FRANCESCATTI

I.

EDOUARD LALO, Op. 21
(1823-1892)

© Copyright 1957 by International Music Company, New York City

D

II.
SCHERZANDO

III.
INTERMEZZO

Allegretto non troppo.($\flat$=76)

IV.

V.
RONDO

F

*) Possible cut.
1377

*) End of possible cut.

CHAMBER ⬥IMC⬥ MUSIC

PIANO TRIOS
(Violin, Cello and Piano)

ARENSKY, Anton
Op. 32. Trio in d minor

BACH, Johann Christian
Trio in D major (RIEMANN -LYMAN)

BEETHOVEN, Ludwig van
Six Celebrated Trios
CONTENTS: Op. 1, Nos. 1 & 3; Op. 11; Op. 70, No. 1;
Op. 97; 10 Variations (KAKADU).
  Viola part (to replace the Cello) (ALTMANN)
Op. 11. Trio in B flat for Piano, Clarinet
  (or Violin) and Cello
Op. 38. Trio in E flat for Piano, Clarinet
  (or Violin) and Cello
Op. 56. Triple concerto in C major for
  Violin, Cello, Piano and Orchestra.
  The set consists of 3 Solo parts (Violin
  edited by DAVID OISTRAKH, Cello
  by LEONARD ROSE) and a score (of
  the same size) containing 3 Solo instruments and a 2nd Piano part (reduction
  of the Orchestra). Thus, for the first
  time this Concerto can be performed by
  the 3 Solo instruments with 2nd Piano
  in place of the Orchestra

BRAHMS, Johannes
Op. 40. Trio in E flat major for Piano,
  Violin and Horn (or Viola or Cello)
Op. 8. Trio No. 1 in B major
Op. 87. Trio No. 2 in C major
Op. 101. Trio No. 3 in c minor
Op. 102. Double Concerto in a minor
  (FRANCESCATTI-FOURNIER)
Viola Part Only (to replace cello) (VIELAND)
Op. 114. Trio in a minor for Piano,
  Clarinet (or Violin or Viola) and Cello

BUXTEHUDE, Dietrich
Op. 2, No. 2. Sonata in D major (SEIFFERT)
Op. 2, No. 6. Sonata in E major (DOEBEREINER)

DVOŘÁK, Antonin
Op. 26. Trio in g minor
Op. 65. Trio in f minor
Op. 90. Trio in e minor ("Dumky")

GLINKA, Michael
Trio Pathétique in d. (Orig. for Clar, Bsn & Po)

HAYDN, Franz Joseph
Five Celebrated Trios
  (Hoboken Listing XV, No. 3; 21; 24; 25; 26)

d'INDY, Vincent
Op. 29. Trio for Piano, Clarinet (or Violin),
  and Cello

LOEILLET, Jean-Baptiste
Sonata in b minor (BEON)
Sonata in G major (BEON)

LOTTI, Antonio
Sonata in G (with 2nd Cello ad lib.)
  (STUTCH-VIELAND)

MOZART, Wolfgang Amadeus
Seven Trios. (DAVID)

RACHMANINOFF, Sergei
Op. 9. Trio Elégiaque

SCHUBERT, Franz
Op. 148. Nocturne in Eb (with Viola part to replace the Cello)
  (KLENGEL-VIELAND)

SCHUMANN, Robert
Op. 88. Fantasy Pieces

SHOSTAKOVICH, Dmitri
Op. 67. Trio in e minor

VIOLIN, CELLO AND PIANO (cont'd)

SMETANA, Bedrich
Op. 15. Trio in g minor

TCHAIKOVSKY, Peter I.
Op. 50. Trio in a minor

VITALI, Giovanni Battista
Op. 4, No. 9. Sonata (HINNENTHAL)

VIVALDI, Antonio
Op. 20/2. Concerto in B flat (Originally for
  Violin, Cello and Orchestra) F.IV, No. 2
  (GINGOLD-NELSOVA-FÜSSL)
Sonata in c. F.XVI, n.1. (GHEDINI)
Pastorale from Rin. Op. 13, N.4 for Piano,
  Flute (or Violin) and Cello (UPMEYER)

WEBER, Carl Maria von
Op. 63. Trio in g min. for Piano, Flute (or Violin)
  and Cello

VIOLIN, VIOLA AND PIANO

BACH, Carl Philipp Emanuel
Trio No. 1 in D major (PICCIOLI)
Trio No. 2 in a minor (PICCIOLI)
Trio No. 3 in G major (PICCIOLI)

BEETHOVEN, Ludwig van
6 Celebrated Trios for Violin, Cello & Piano:
  Viola Part Only (to replace the Cello)
  (ALTMANN)

BRAHMS, Johannes
Op. 102. Double Concerto in a minor for Violin,
  Cello and Piano (FRANCESCATTI-FOURNIER):
  Viola Part Only (to replace the Cello) (VIELAND)
Op. 40. Trio in E flat major

HANDEL, George Frederick
Op. 2, No. 3. Sonata in F (VIELAND)
Op. 2, No. 8 Sonata in g (VIELAND)

KHACHATURIAN, Aram
Trio

LOEILLET, Jean-Baptiste
Sonata in D major (BEON-VIELAND)
Sonata in G major (BEON-VIELAND)

LOTTI, Antonio
Sonata in G (with 2nd Cello ad lib.)
  (STUTCH-VIELAND)

MOZART, Wolfgang Amadeus
Symphonie Concertante in E flat (K.364)
  With Cadenzas by MOZART and
  HELLMESBERGER
Trio in E flat major (K.498) for Clarinet
  (or Violin), Viola and Piano

PURCELL, Henry
Golden Sonata in F (WOEHL-VIELAND)

SCHUBERT, Franz
Op. 148. Nocturne in Eb (with Viola part
  to replace the Cello) (KLENGEL-VIELAND)

SCHUMANN, Robert
Op. 132. Fairy Tales

VIOLA, CELLO AND PIANO

BACH, Carl Philipp Emanuel
6 Sonatas (PICCIOLI)
Trio in F major (PICCIOLI)

BRAHMS, Johannes
Op. 114. Trio in a minor for Piano, Clarinet
  (or Violin or Viola) and Cello

VIOLA, BASS AND PIANO

DITTERSDORF, Carl Ditters von
Sinfonie Concertante in D (SANKEY) Standard and solo tuning.
  (New edition based on the original manuscript)

INTERNATIONAL MUSIC COMPANY

5 WEST 37th STREET   Complete catalog sent free on request   **NEW YORK, N. Y. 10018**

hc

No. 55-88